better together*

*This book is best read together, grownup and kid.

 akidsco.com

a
kids
book
about

a kids book about

bullying

by Elizabeth Tom

A Kids Co.
Editor Jelani Memory
Designer Duke Stebbins
Creative Director Rick DeLucco
Studio Manager Kenya Feldes
Sales Director Melanie Wilkins
Head of Books Jennifer Goldstein
CEO and Founder Jelani Memory

DK
Editor Emma Roberts
Senior Production Editor Jennifer Murray
Senior Production Controller Louise Minihane
Senior Acquisitions Editor Katy Flint
Acquisitions Project Editor Sara Forster
Managing Art Editor Vicky Short
Publishing Director Mark Searle
DK would like to thank Natasha Devon

This American Edition, 2024
Published in the United States by DK Publishing
1745 Broadway, 20th Floor, New York, NY 10019

DK, a Division of Penguin Random House LLC
Text and design copyright © 2020 by A Kids Book About, Inc.
A Kids Book About, Kids Are Ready, and the colophon 'a' are trademarks of A Kids Book About, Inc.
24 25 26 27 10 9 8 7 6 5 4 3 2 1
001-339427-July/2024

All rights reserved. Without limiting the rights under the copyright reserved above,
no part of this publication may be reproduced, stored in or introduced into a retrieval system,
or transmitted, in any form, or by any means (electronic, mechanical, photocopying, recording,
or otherwise), without the prior written permission of the copyright owner.
Published in Great Britain by Dorling Kindersley Limited.

A catalog record for this book is available from the Library of Congress.
ISBN: 978-0-5938-4385-7

DK books are available at special discounts when purchased in bulk for
sales promotions, premiums, fund-raising, or educational use. For details, contact:
DK Publishing Special Markets, 1745 Broadway, 20th Floor, New York, NY 10019, or SpecialSales@dk.com

Printed and bound in China

www.dk.com

akidsco.com

This book was made with Forest
Stewardship Council™ certified
paper – one small step in DK's
commitment to a sustainable future.
**Learn more at www.dk.com/uk/
information/sustainability**

Thank you, Mrs. J, for all the impact you had on my life.

Intro
for grownups

My dad said once, "You need a point A for there to be a point B." Each challenge we face shapes us into who and what we are today. For me, one of the challenges I faced was being bullied. I decided to become like the bully because I thought that would make it better. I thought hurting people was going to solve my hurt. But, it just made it way worse.

The truth is, we all have self-doubt and insecurity at some point, and many of us are hurting inside. How we deal with all of it is unique to each of us. Eventually, I learned only love can heal—and for me, putting my faith and trust in a higher power taught me that.

When I wrote this book, it brought back a lot of really hard memories. But even though it was difficult, I'm glad I did it. My hope is that it helps the kid in your life—whether they're hurting inside and don't know what to do, or they know someone who needs their understanding and support.

Hi, my name is Elizabeth Tom.

You can call me " 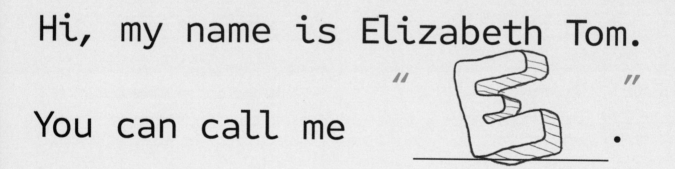 ".

I'm **14** years old.

卌 卌 IIII

And I'm funny. I like basketball,
horseback riding, and laughing
a lot.

I also like food a lot.
Like, **A LOT**! Pizza and tacos
are my favorites.

I'm a normal kid,

but I'm also different.

I have a disability called
Ataxic Cerebral Palsy.

Ataxic Cerebral Palsy is a condition that affects motor function.

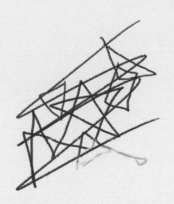

That means my muscles don't always work the way they're supposed to.

Which means I don't always
talk like other kids.

And it's hard for people
to understand me sometimes.

But not when I write,
because I'm an _incredible_ writer!

This is my book about

bullying. *

* Bullying is when someone deliberately harms
or frightens someone else, or tries to make
them do something they don't want to do.

10

It's about
how it feels
when you're bullied,

how to deal
with bullying,

and
what life looks like
after being bullied.

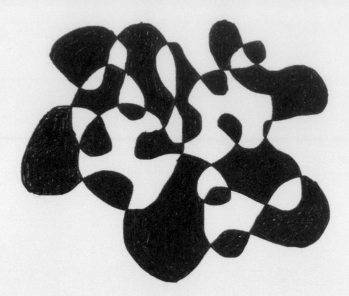

Most people think bullying is when kids at school push, hurt, or make fun of you.

And <u>sometimes</u> it is.

But it's

much

more than that.

Bullying can happen
among grownups,
it can happen at home,
and it can even happen
when you don't realize
it is happening...

I believe bullying is:

~~####~~ when someone hurts someone
else because they are hurting inside.*

* But that doesn't make bullying OK.

When I was in the 4th grade,
I felt like I was treated
differently because of
my disability.

Sometimes it was small things,
like how my teacher treated me.

Even though I could do all the
work the rest of the kids in
my class could do.

$18 \times 2 - 7.5 = 28.5$

Other times,
it was in bigger ways,
like being excluded
by the other kids.

I didn't like it,
but most of the time I was
fine, and I just got over it.

There were times when it got even worse though, and I would be taunted and called names.

I *really* didn't like those times,
but I didn't know what to do.

I didn't tell my parents.

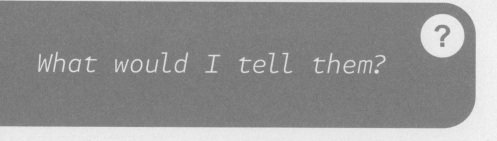

What would I tell them? **?**

I thought I was going to be <u>fine</u>.

(But, I wasn't.)

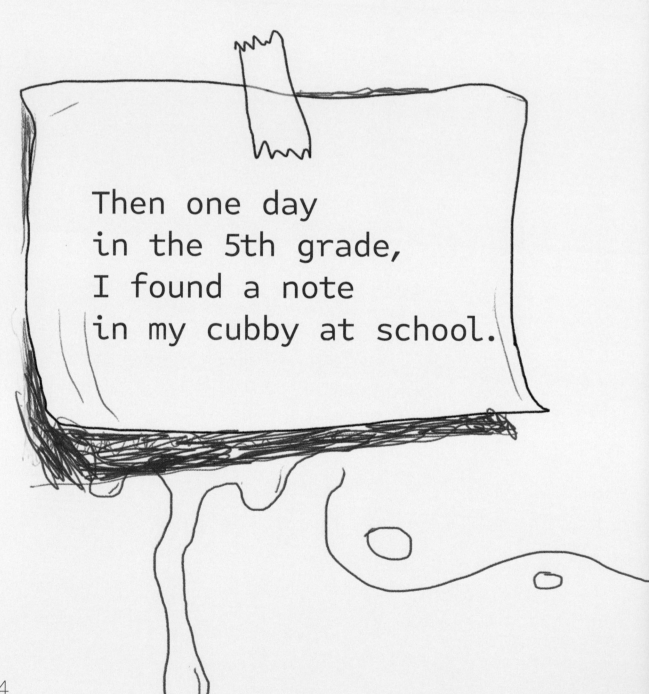

Then one day
in the 5th grade,
I found a note
in my cubby at school.

I can't even tell you
everything the note said
because it was *that* bad.

But it did say

no one loved me

or ever would

and everyone who said they did

was lying to me.

27

At first I felt...

I wanted to punch the kid who wrote it.

Then I felt...

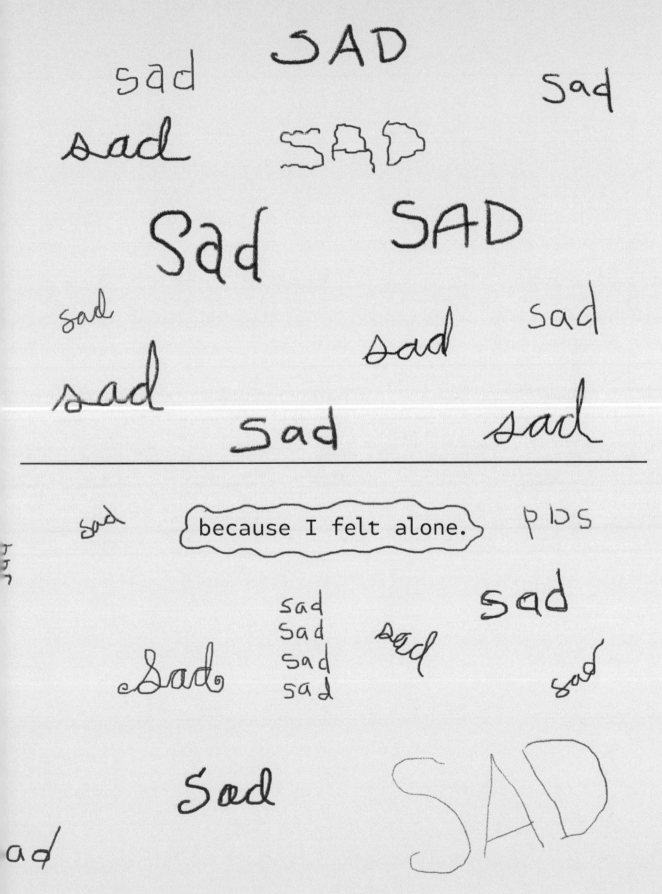

sad SAD sad
sad SAD
Sad SAD
sad sad sad
sad
Sad sad

because I felt alone. pos

sad sad
sad sad
Sad sad
Sad sad
Sad sad

Sad SAD

ad

31

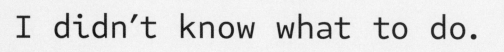

I didn't know what to do.

- Would no one ever really love me?

- Was no one really my friend?

- Could I trust anyone?

Even though I felt angry and sad and didn't know what to do...

I did do <u>one</u> thing.

I showed the note to my friend.

And my friend did something
small, but **incredible.**

She told me to tell the teacher.

You see, I could have never
let anyone see the note.

I could have stuffed down
my feelings.

And I could have pretended
like it never happened.

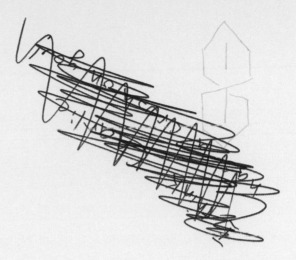

And my friend could have
told me not to show anyone,
especially the teacher.

Or she could have thought
I just made it all up.

But when she _encouraged_ me to tell the _teacher_ , she gave me _permission_ and **courage** to not just let it go..

So I told the **teacher** and
showed her the note.

But I didn't STOP there.

I also felt **brave** enough
to tell my mom and dad.
And they helped me.

But, even though I was being bullied, it was hard for me to accept that I was.

I couldn't bring myself to admit I was being bullied until I was in 6th grade.

The thing about bullying is,
it can make you doubt yourself.

It's not always clear what's happening.

Sometimes it feels bad,
but you can make excuses
and try to brush it off.

But that doesn't make
anything better.

When you get bullied, it can make you feel:

lonely, scared, sad, angry,

embarrassed, different,

and a hundred other feelings.

It's not always the same for every person.

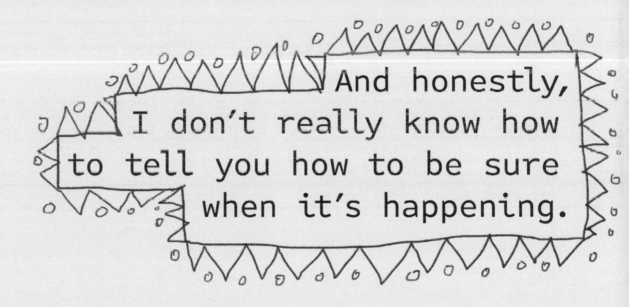

And honestly, I don't really know how to tell you how to be sure when it's happening.

But, I do know
the effects and the feelings
don't just go away after it stops.

Sometimes they stay with you

...for years.

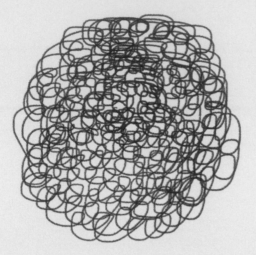

When I was getting bullied, it
made me feel _different_ .

I started to bully other kids
so I didn't feel so _different_ .

I didn't even realize that
was what I was doing.

I was just hurt and I wanted
to make other people hurt.

If bullying is anything,
it's that.*

* But, it's still not OK!

Bullying is hurt people,

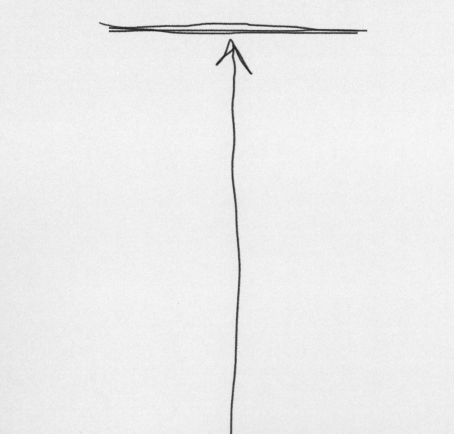

who hurt other people.

So, what can you do?

You can't always stop the bullying.

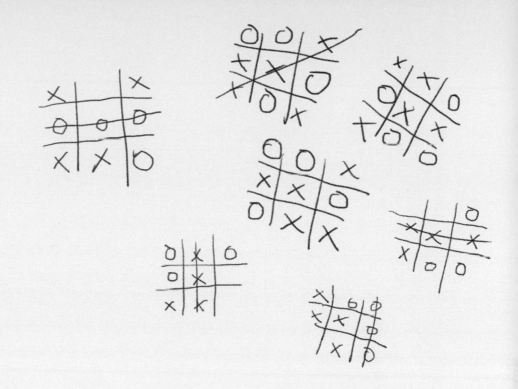

You *can* tell a safe person.

Like I did.

Then you won't be alone,
and you'll have help.

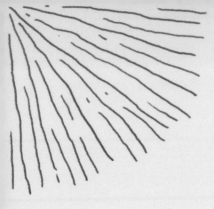

And if you're hurting
because you're being bullied...

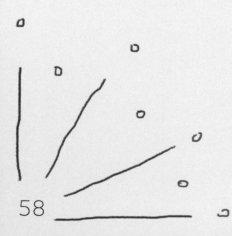

don't try to make
others hurt, too.

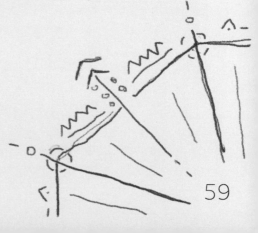

Treat others
how you want to be treated.

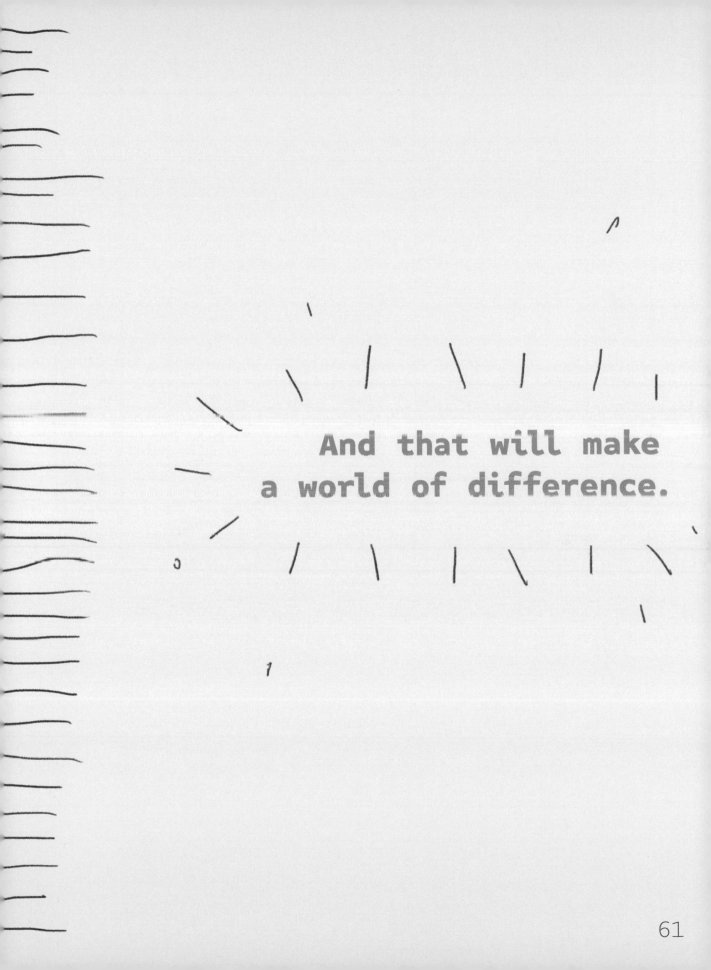

And that will make
a world of difference.

Outro
for grownups

Wow, that was heavy stuff, huh? You're probably asking yourself, "What now, E?"

I'm glad you asked. I didn't get here all on my own. I had help. So if the kid in your life knows people who are being picked on, bullied, or not treated right, I'd encourage them to find little ways to make those people feel important. Be their "help." Maybe it is a positive comment, hanging out with them, or maybe it is just being a friend.

The truth is, we all want to feel important and the small things we do can be powerful to another person. When we stick up for someone else, we can change the world!

About The Author

Elizabeth Tom (she/her) is a fun, loving, passionate, loyal person who truly enjoys writing. In 2018, Elizabeth shared her story with her whole church and never could have imagined what was to follow—she was asked to write a book about her personal experience with bullying.

It was a dream come true, but even so, Elizabeth couldn't believe it was happening. Not only would she be an author, but she would have the opportunity to give hope to hurting kids.

Elizabeth wants kids to know that no matter how hurt they are, they are never alone and can ALWAYS ask for help. She hopes this book is only the beginning of her writing career and is excited to see what God has planned for her next.

 @akidsco f @akidsco 🌐 akidsco.com